WHY DO PEOPLE TAKE DRUGS ?

© Aladdin Books 1988

Designed and produced by
Aladdin Books Ltd, 70 Old Compton Street, London W1V 5PA

Editor: Catherine Bradley
Design: Rob Hillier
Illustration: Ron Hayward Associates
Research: Cecilia Weston-Baker
Consultant: Angela Grunsell

Judith Hemming has taught in both primary and secondary schools and has co-authored many books aimed at helping children talk and write about important issues.

Angela Grunsell is an advisory teacher specialising in development education and resources for the primary school age range.

Published in Great Britain in 1988 by
Franklin Watts Ltd, 12a Golden Square, London W1R 4BA

ISBN 0 86313 771 7

Printed in Belgium

Reprinted 1989

"LET'S TALK ABOUT"

WHY DO PEOPLE TAKE DRUGS?

JUDITH HEMMING

Gloucester Press
London · New York · Toronto · Sydney

It's hard to connect eating sweets with tooth decay.

"What does it feel like to want to take drugs?"

Imagine yourself at the checkout counter of a supermarket in front of some sweets. You want some. Adults may have told you that the sugar in sweets gives you a burst of energy which can leave you feeling tired and cross. But you really want them . . .

If you've ever felt like that, then you have some idea of what it's like to want to take pills or drugs. Different kinds of drugs are all around you. Anyone can get into problems with drugs. This book explores why people take drugs.

"What is a drug?"

A drug is anything you put into your body, other than food, that changes the way your body works and makes you feel different. Some drugs are part of most people's lives, like tea or coffee. Other drugs, like alcohol in wine or beer and nicotine in cigarettes, are more powerful.

> The opium poppy contains the drug opium, which can be made into morphine. This is used to relieve pain in hospitals. It is also made into heroin, which is stronger.

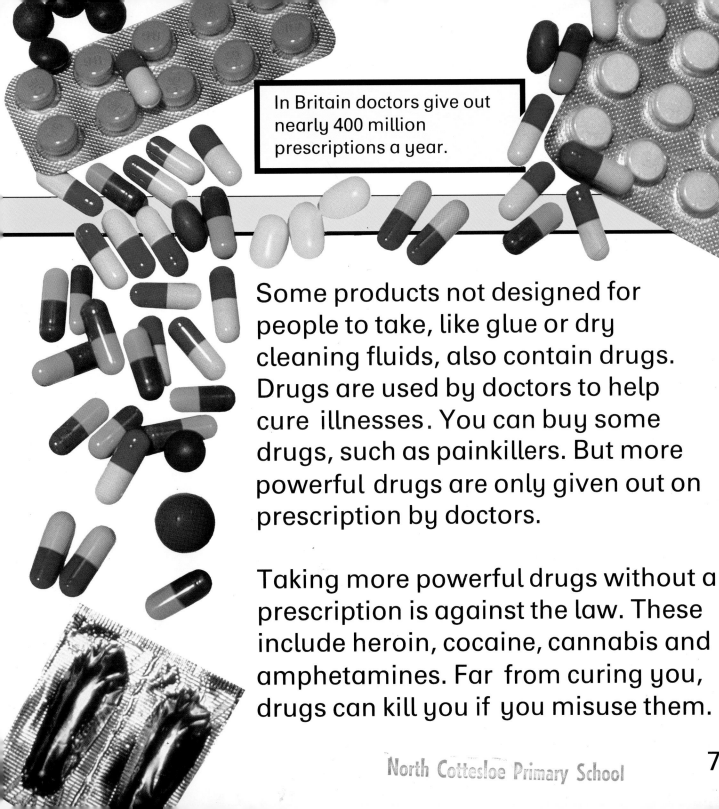

In Britain doctors give out nearly 400 million prescriptions a year.

Some products not designed for people to take, like glue or dry cleaning fluids, also contain drugs. Drugs are used by doctors to help cure illnesses. You can buy some drugs, such as painkillers. But more powerful drugs are only given out on prescription by doctors.

Taking more powerful drugs without a prescription is against the law. These include heroin, cocaine, cannabis and amphetamines. Far from curing you, drugs can kill you if you misuse them.

"How does a drug work? How does it affect your body?"

When you take a drug or medicine it takes time before it starts to have any effect. You swallow a pill and it goes into your stomach. Then it goes into the bloodstream and is pumped by the heart to the brain. The drug travels all over your body.

All drugs act in a similar way. There are many ways of taking drugs from smoking them to eating them. Their effects can last for minutes or many hours. There may be some traces of the drug's effects after several days.

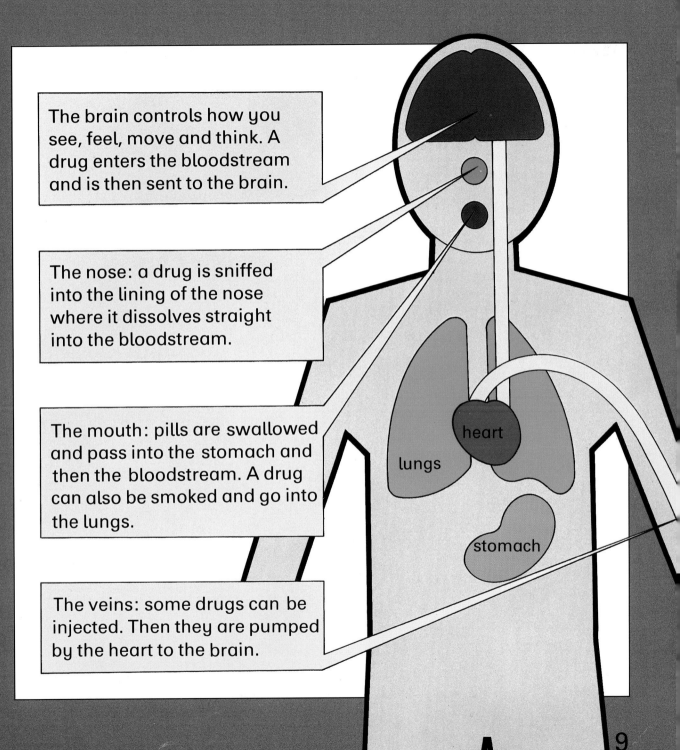

The brain controls how you see, feel, move and think. A drug enters the bloodstream and is then sent to the brain.

The nose: a drug is sniffed into the lining of the nose where it dissolves straight into the bloodstream.

The mouth: pills are swallowed and pass into the stomach and then the bloodstream. A drug can also be smoked and go into the lungs.

The veins: some drugs can be injected. Then they are pumped by the heart to the brain.

heart

lungs

stomach

9

"What about drugs from a doctor?"

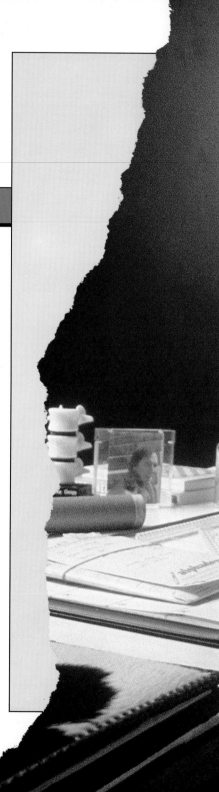

Drugs from a doctor are meant to help people get well if they are ill. In some cases drugs from a doctor help people to stay alive. Doctors are careful to give the right drug and the right amount to each person. Drugs are safe to take as long as you follow the doctor's directions. You must never take medicine that a doctor has prescribed for someone else.

People often expect to be given medicine by a doctor to make them feel better.

Enjoying yourself at a party can be good fun.
This is one way to feel good. But some people
are not able enjoy themselves in this way.
They may turn to drugs.

"Why do people take drugs?"

People end up taking drugs for many different reasons. Maybe they feel they need something to help them with their problems and make them feel good. Drugs can feel like a delight at first but later like a nightmare.

If you're feeling unhappy, you often need someone to talk to and share your problems. Maybe you don't feel you can turn to anyone or you think you can sort out your problems yourself. This may make you the kind of person who might rely on drugs.

"Who takes drugs?"

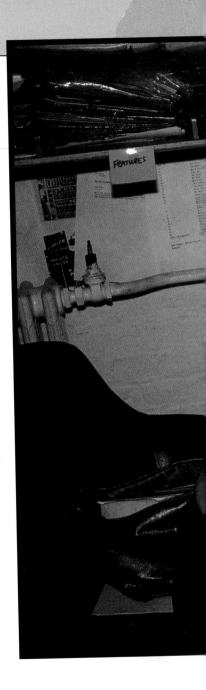

Most people in the world take some kind of drug. Most countries allow people to use alcohol and tobacco. Some countries ban alcohol for religious reasons because it affects your mind and body.

You can end up relying on a drug without realising what you are doing. For example, nearly a million people (mainly women) in Britain are in the habit of taking Valium, a drug given by doctors to help them relax. Giving it up can be very difficult.

Women and men often turn to medicines, drink or drugs when they cannot cope with their jobs or home life. Maybe the job or home should be changed.

Those who seem successful are just as likely to take drugs as those who feel they cannot cope. Some young business women and men use an expensive drug, cocaine, because they think it will improve their performance. Young people in big cities are the ones most likely to try out illegal drugs. They may find taking risks with drugs exciting. They will come across them at parties, clubs and on the streets.

Some teenage boys and girls use glue because it is cheap and easy to get hold of. Sniffing solvents, such as glue, is not against the law. Selling solvents to young people if you think they are going to sniff them is illegal. But it's difficult to stop shopkeepers from selling them.

Sniffing solvents is very dangerous. Some aerosols can kill people if they spray them down their throat.

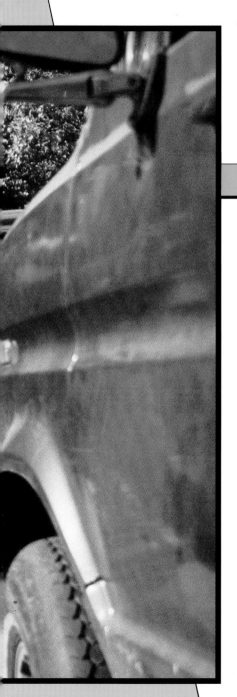

"What is the cost of taking drugs?"

If you take drugs you might get so used to them that they become a habit. You could come to rely on them so much that you find it difficult to give them up. Heavy users of heroin can get desperate without it. In fact it may become the most important thing in their lives. They have to buy the drugs from dealers, who are part of a criminal network of drug traders.

Buying drugs is expensive. It can cost more than £10 a day to buy heroin from a dealer.

"How difficult is it to give up drugs?"

People have to want to stop taking drugs. It's not enough that their friends and family want them to stop. For those who rely on drugs, the first step is to make sure that they get lots of rest, food and help, while their body gets rid of the drug. They may feel ill for a while.

Giving up drugs can be hard. People need support from friends and others to do it. There are many drug centres, hospitals, self help groups, telephone hot lines and specialists to turn to.

20

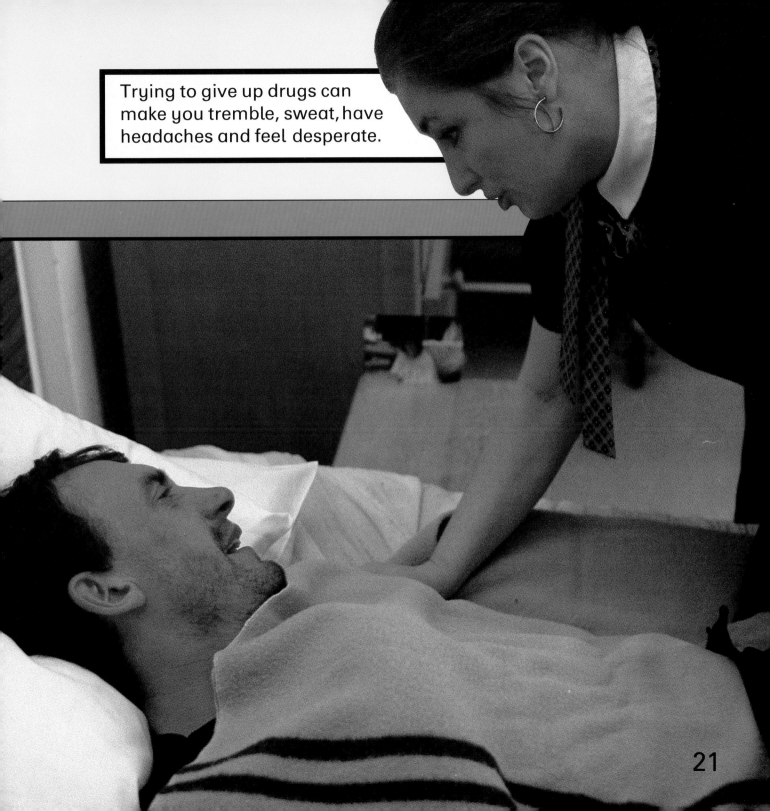

Trying to give up drugs can make you tremble, sweat, have headaches and feel desperate.

21

"Why is it hard to say 'no' to drugs?"

You've all come across crazes at school. Suddenly everyone has to have a care bear or a computer game. If you haven't got one, you feel left out.

It's the same with drugs. It's hard to say no if all your friends are doing it or they dare you to do it. For example, if a friend is using drugs to improve her or his ability in sport, it's tempting to do the same. Some drugs can help you enjoy yourself or concentrate on your work better. But those feelings won't last.

North Cottesloe Primary School

If your friends or family smoke, you may feel you're missing out on something. In fact learning to smoke can be unpleasant.

23

Perhaps you or someone you know is worried about drugs. The most important thing to do if you need help is talk to someone you trust and tell them about your worries.

"What are the dangers of taking drugs?"

Certain drugs can seriously damage your health. If you sniff glue, you can feel very ill. You are also more likely to have an accident and choke. Using heroin can result in many serious problems, including malnutrition. People who smoke cigarettes run the risk of getting bronchitis, cancer and heart attacks.

It's not always easy to tell if someone is on drugs. Some people can carry on their life without anyone else knowing that they are using them.

"How can you stop people from taking illegal drugs?"

One solution is to warn people of the dangers of taking drugs. Governments use advertisements and education programmes but they do not stop some people from trying them.

Another solution would be to stop the drugs from reaching Europe and North America. But the countries that produce cannabis, heroin and cocaine are poor. The farmers need the income. Drug smugglers make huge profits and bribe customs officers and police to turn a blind eye to the trade.

Every time drug smugglers are arrested by the police, there are always several people willing to take their place.

"What next?"

For some people life is unfair and difficult, and drugs seem to be the answer to their problems. If someone is relying on drugs, the most important thing is to stop taking drugs and the next most important thing is learning how to carry on living without using them.

We all need to learn safe ways to feel calm, energetic or confident. We need to know that difficult moments will pass. We need to like ourselves enough to look after ourselves.

COKE
IS NOT IT
NOTTINGHILL CARNIVAL
1986

KEEP OFF THE
DRUG
SPECIAL BRANCH IS
MAKING NO JOKE
SO STAY OFF THE COKE

COKE IS THE REAL THING
EX. ADDICT ↓

Coke is short for cocaine.
People can help each other
cope without drugs.

29

"What can I do?"

Maybe you want to carry on talking and thinking about the problem of drugs. The best thing is to find a grown up to talk to. If you're lucky this will be a parent, teacher or neighbour.

Other places to turn to are listed below. Families Anonymous helps people who have someone in their family on drugs. ChildLine is for children to turn to if they can't find anyone to talk about problems, including drugs.

Addresses for more information

Families Anonymous	ChildLine	Institute for the Study
5-7 Parson's Green	Freepost 111	of Drug Dependence
London SW6 4UL	London EC4B 4BB	1-4 Hatton Place
Tel: 01 731 8060	Tel: 0800 1111	London EC1N 8ND

What the words mean

Alcohol: A liquid made by fermenting sugar. It is in cider, beer, wine and spirits.

Amphetamines: Pills made from chemicals which make people feel energetic and happy.

Cannabis: A drug made from the leaves or flowering top of a plant that grows in many parts of the world and can be smoked.

Cocaine: A drug made from the coca plant that grows mainly in South America.

Heroin: A white powder made from the opium poppy, which grows in parts of Asia and in Central America.

Index

a alcohol 6, 14, 15, 31
amphetamines 7, 31

c cannabis 7, 26, 31
cigarettes 6, 14, 21, 25
cocaine 7, 16, 26, 29, 31

g glue 7, 16, 17, 25

h heroin 6, 7, 19, 25 26, 31

m medicines and

prescription drugs 7, 8, 10, 11, 15
morphine 6

o opium 6

s saying "no" to drugs 22, 23, 24, 25 26, 28

v Valium, 14

w why people take drugs 5, 10, 12, 13, 15, 16, 22, 23, 25, 28

Photographic Credits:
Cover and page 19: Sally and Richard Greenhill; pages 11, 17, 23 and 29: Network

Photographers; pages 4, 6, 7, and 14: Rex Features; page 18 and 27: David Browne; page 24: Janine Weidel.

PRINTED IN BELGIUM BY
proost
INTERNATIONAL BOOK PRODUCTION